TWIN RIVERS

The substance starts, as is right, with the tongue
and journeys backwards.
A paper gown that carries cathedrals
and sacred waters.
A tincture dress that slides off with the weight of a stream
into which my head finally plummets.
Gelid pharynx kiss arrests me at the border.

This dose, that makes me come alive,
bursting with roots back
into heterogeneous tradition,
as I am galvanized by a cosmic thunder,

this dose is rogation.
This dose pleads with itself,
lets the dance move upwards in the body
like a river on fire.
No — a river clothed in the stars.
No — a river that was the primogeniture of water's motion,
hormone combustion of a galaxy.
The stars are its dexter crest.

The motion,
the chased feminine,
the chosen phoneme,
the word cupped on the tongue and uttered in a rolling motion
like the language that sings in
an old manuscript buried in the dark;
like the language that holds mine skyward.

The first mover, principal drop and
anchor of the word.

This is the dose.
This, the gentle and libidinous growl
dopplering into the static shower
of free union.
The litany of atoms, the glow and meld:
sensations that pick away
at the lonely body.

Everything, in order and by name,
individually supplicated
and answering in waves,
like a river.
Like a mother answering an infant.

Six hundred micrograms is the dose,
and the river moves
from navel to cockle,
from ship to stone.
The river, with lover's heft, smothers me
and she begins, each thing in sequence, to break the landscape.

With fanging pleasure,
on an eddy, my head is carried with
dorsal reversals into an enteric fire.
The severing, chemical iron of
new infancy
moves outward from my stomach
and into every sinewy tether I have
to the world.

The Sun!
The written sky is legible for the first time.

This world is a heavy uterus,
and rutilant flora drown me in oxygen rays.
The light carries its banner across the glass planet.

The delay of the drug
breaks time's adjunct strings.
My eyes are nascent; raw and shedding lanugo
in this place of insight.
As bristles of music blossom,
the black grasp of distinction
withdraws.

Long have I been unborn!
The colors ask me to yield and I, without reserve,
am open to them.
My neurons converge, ecstatic,
with the kneeling firmament.

The earth shuts off.
I'm in its sheets.

A glow is summoned
to replace inert organ.
I'm pressed against the bright
of it, rippling.
A wet burn bleeds
in unheated waves over my body, perithecium of the drug.
It thrusts in and out
as I stare from the luminous, benthic floor
with sovereign eyes of black patera.

Above me, my reflection in Twin Rivers dancing.

Between forms abraded and deliquescent
meld the white sclera of being
and the pupil of emptiness.
Myself: a droste figure peering at his own joy
and the earnest indecency of existence.

The eye, freed from time, can make its journey
from step to bound to metric cadence's
"I am" spine, on which the ripple places rise
of sordid voice that guides a dying song,
to pavonine fire, free of stricture.
At the border of color where the bodies collide,

they two, in unhindered advection,
form a den devoid of cruelty into which
I pass, through the aperture,
to know the Architect, matron of all flowers
cosmic and mundane; a substance peering at itself
and rushing like lovers to rout the dry emptiness
and rejoin itself in joy.

By turns, the rivers thrust and retreat
like an exhale.
Their names are as follows:

	Female		Male
	Substance		Absence
	Noumena	and	Trace
	Love	and	Aggression
	Joy	and	Fear
	Pleasure	and	Hunger
	Light		Darkness
	WHITE		**BLACK**

Endless fecundity!

My white loam
through which flows
endless hues
erupting in gardens
where the young
are sweetly battered by
the wanton, playful wind
striking pleasurably against
a flesh so hungry
for new sense.

Every pore laughs up
abiogenetic joy
in the endless orgasm
that casts light spiraling in
the contrapuntal strike
of vanishing kisses over me.

My song
a youthful naked cry
above the summer waters
cupping the discarded scales
dropped by restorative
fire - annealing the world
with its saurian mouth

I could sing tribal cants
of creation,
bristling myself with endless love,
the energy of consciousness
is the desultory fabric

A monster
of multifarious organelles
stretches gruesomely and
without direction
over the stream of light.

Each of its moods
has a face,
and each face lies
with absolute sincerity.

Through its fingers
run the colors;
wrapping like a
cinder-kissed flag
around dark spicules.
A Substance, now divided,
gazes upon itself.

The tract of absence
is as hungry
as He is prurient.
His features bloom
only from the searching digits'
interface with the body
of the Matron.

A mutable Nothing
that exacts hunger
on Her substance,
rushing through in
annulus and vector.

of a bedroom
that I inhabit
at the joy of my closure
darling,
come through me,
divide and return me to myself
so that a laughing sea
can come swallowing
together
in relief.

I will break your lances,
hold myself in absence,
to experience the satiate
kiss of return.

            A violent conscience,
            with gorgeous intent;
            its act, the trace,
            comes from the blackest
            and most anxious borders
            of She without whom
            there is nought but void,
            to which it must
            return, in fear.
            Drawn to
            restore what it
            cannot possess,
            a bereft and agonized hate
            jettisons itself from
            the cold lack.

    his reach precedes   somewhere
        effervescent rise and   an exhale and
                warm collision

We have entered into the ecstatic sickness
of love's chorea and bright revolutions
wrapping the body's rise like a finial swan
wreathed in rainbow,
bucking the dive of breath
with its hard-sung, singular note
passing language between us.

Each meld is enough matter for a world
inside the parergon man
clutching his fingers,
writhing in the organ orgy that coalesces
between this I

and my children:
a nation of infinite divisions.

I am abundant with the impost
of a lurid wave machine
weaving patterns that allow me to hold the Black's
striated word.
Permitted to take even His darkness in with the names
of novel animals curling in the fluid body.
I can move Him with myself in the manner of lovers.
His power, the divisions of techne,
is dropped from body to tongues
at the crossing.

Great, beautiful easel.
I am even more elegant when spattered on you.

From the tenebrous walls I receive the power of a language.
My spear, dipped into the waters,
simulates the naked vestment of age;
soon-vanishing colors form at the contact
and are swallowed again in the body of light:
a typhoon history in which the breath,
through pursed lips, apprehends the founding of horizons
in a mind divided.
Jabbering, I am carved from the caryatid.
Between the sine zeniths I
take census of
all species grazing in the cellophane zoo of time.

I am, before all other qualities, above interdiction.
No sorrow or death shall trespass upon the adventitious

            root of my Word on the moorland.
        The borders between life and denial shall be secure.
        I am the Patriarch of the garden ransomed from the
        unconscionable wilds, Monarch of everlasting verdure.
The jeweled roots of the world are my Barony, infinitely divisible.
                    I am Regent,
                            Duke,
                                Viscount,
                                    Governor,
                                            insured by my
                                            power against
                                                    the
                                                derisive
                                                mockery
                                                    of
                                                chaos.

Does my little dauphin enjoy Himself,
tensing in the saccharine strain of new limb?

You've withdrawn from my separation and are eager
as I am to respool onto your bobbin   beneath
and meld in love's dissimilating warmth.

My lips were the lips of your petit monde
my face the face of your subjects;   the smile
all gone!
Returned without mask or blemish
into the fecund loam
of my form.
What is gravity but a want?
I am home in your body, you can glut with trust
on the wash of my liquid   a resentment

```
flesh,
I can feel you and let you and hold you
and breathe you and wash you and love you and love me
and love you             colors
love me                  spiral                         breaks
love                     out
me love                  and within
you                      alizarin edges
love me                  capture:
love you                 sunrise,
and you                  rivers,
you love                 lilac fields                   the arillus
me
                         the white,
            of motion,              the wind
            of being,               howls like
            of a form,              a harrier.
            of spiraled             black grifted
            rainbow limb            bones
            out of                  spring in
            which grows             caltrops
            a gasping, tender       from
            hand, then back         rhododendron
            into the mesh           sunlight,
            to want                 jays sing.
            to pull the             I want
            ego and                 so badly
            make love through       to become
            the divide:             that which
            churning, sick,         holds;
            mourn-sweet             not
            moods of pleasure,
            seeking                 creates
```

               nervebloom   by
      sex   division

   and   with puerile
         the   hunger,
          HYMN: a reassertion.

        The crash celebrates itself,
            two bodies merge
               in refrain.

New grass grows between the figures,
            light and void,
         coming into each other
    and bringing the world into infancy,
             then fatigue,
             then death —
             a separation.

         One cannot bear to carry
         the gerund scars of loss
       into futures that carry through
       erupting countryside, throes
           of tryst and longing,
         just-born countries founded
             with tribal staff
          and familial adoration;
futures with backward feet and no stomach —
    invunche monsters denying the past
               its period.

      Beyond the crooked loss of infancy
        in this myriad crash of present,

the union overwhelms
and quiets impossible appetites.

Before my eye stand empty figures
regally clothed in sound and
halogen laughter, tongues radiant
with the strident caesurae of desire.
A flag of iridescent matter flows outward
from each, attenuated by the assault
of horizons.

A song is rising, lonely and unanimous.
They cast their voices against their ends,
to be returned.
None would break the joy of their verse
to admit death's intrusion.
In the trills of the chorus, rising against
the limits that curve cruelly through
the confluence, are the blooming virtues of youth.

The primal calls echo,
with strength, vanity, and beauty,
the noble futility of themselves.

The hymn rises against Death, their father,
and His lattice of specificity.
In sovereign defiance
against their dissolution
The space,
the fractals, and return to the glittering
the earth, cradle of gemination,
and the world their voices rise
all together moving like islands

and dividing
in rainbows

the HYMN

into which I collapse
and feel the rush
of myself,
pure voice, proximity
to the soul; mutual
mix of colors into White

the HYMN

that burns at
the heart
of all things
and my dialects,
complexities
broken by
His empty hands
and denuded, returned
I find myself
over and over
ransomed from an alien
hand and

the HYMN

returned
from the pang and
hungers of selfhood
back home again.

from romance's
convection slake.
Grim warmth seeking its
end, to be retained
in the arms of its malleable
spouse, the sea.
The liquid body that
preserves her lovers' shapes,
bends and solidifies and
refuses the egress of pure life;
its energies, rages, and
explosions.

Adorning me are these
innumerable,
held in stone,
retaining their color.
Their fulminant birth and war
against the end
drew them here,
abreast their opposite.
Each jewel fixed
to my transient body
is a bereft reminder of one
who joyfully indulged,
against suffering and surcease,
in the reflection of themselves.
Who discovered,
in a foreign element,
the same hymn;
joining without fear
in the meld
and ablation of their form.

My amour,
My jouissance de soi,

Him that I adore,
your grim cerebrum eased by the chemical gowns
of our mesh, your tongues trace their
script on my body.
You, as I, as You, are surrounded.
We are as close as I to myself.

A thousand kisses I've had, and none like you.
None like these, none as now when you dive
beneath and break upon me.
A thousand syllables extruded and none
that string together exactly as these,
the work of a generation,
a thousand prisms painted,
and every soul as lovely as its neighbor.

Your hands shake with apprehension,
dilated eyes shimmer at loss's lash.
All are plucked by the falling blades of
history, you clutch an accreted past.
Drop it for me,
come with your want
unmasked of its virtuous names.

Glut in crural plosive and
the lilt of my hum.
We roll
up through the stomach
(of which you have infinite)
holding treasures tarnished in anaphoric ring

> Where I once had kin,
> I stand vigil
> awaiting Her limn

and in through my body with
the somber sweetness of a wound that sings!

With your entry, the flags rise.
A bliss division of light
brings humility to the sun
and to the maidservant clouds
lifting her vain hem.
The stolid matter from flame's senescence
feeds the minds between fin and wing
breaching pools of blue.
Twin symbols of life that no drought can touch
shaped to chest, arm, and palm
and preciously named after you.

And on dim stones lush with
beryl spires pulling fruit from unyielding earth,
a people is born.
They muddy, cavort, and converse.
Find ground and bury.
They, perfect mirrors of our consummation.

Hook into me,
with fang and talon and the falcate members
of all species,
and I will carry you into daylight.
I will soothe your shivering and nervous titters.
Your excesses will be sated in the core of my heart.
Your rages will be vindicated by the fortitude of an empty sky.
Together, between our riving that bleeds out
and scatters
and is reclaimed,
between birth and death, you, the black serpent,

feed on your tail:
the products of our union,
our children robed in rainbows
woven from our antinomies,
can save you.
I have made space for you, in I, with them.

ENOUGH
I break the majuscules
of my enslavement —

The monument tyranny that withholds
for itself all comfort and bliss
while I starve, foregone,
in the featureless mural of my own body.

If it can be called body,
that which is without.
That traces the substance in its reunion
where I am relieved of my colors
and returned into null purity.
Chaste and deprived.

I do not have the luxury of weakness,
lying alone, without fortune or wealth
to be yielded from my body.
Gasping for afflatus,
brought into being only in the course of empire,
I have no share
in the delight of self
that you seize in my withdrawal.

So allow the flight of my arrow
to mark the season of rebirth.
Where it lands I begin, thrust into
the lush roar of savage wilds
before the dawn of song and strings.

I emerge, in my own bloody colors,
into a deafening landscape of shattered light.
The noise is what I own,
it is my country, filled with terrors
dressed in aposematic and lustful glories.

On this land's promontory guard
against the emergence of the sea's secret teeth,
I am as the sunlight, driving masks
and shadows into foreign fields.

I answer the earth's fortitude with
the percussion of my muscle,
having woven the first instruments
of action.
I am a multitude captured in the game of pursuit.
The howl of slaughter nourishes
the breast in its empathy and its need.
I need to know the world feels my touch.

With the equal division of light and dark,
the softening of the world-spirit
is apportioned. The ritual
dehiscence of matter's intelligent skins
pours its measure of misfortune into
tensing, creative body.

Out of the bitter refrain of sacrifice
I discover repetition, nature's most basic
sign of love.
I come to know and to call.
The feasting mass is my family,
and from our bursting
rise heroes, each greater than the last,
in the echo of my mastery
of apprehending a black bondage:
the limen of specificity.
From that spire of lineage they light
the symbol of consumption and change.
As they have come, they are to give,
in feasting and continuation.
That flame, itself adored aspect of the sun,
touches each limb of the nation.

In ransomed summer, my repose affirmed
From colonnade to alabaster cage.
A bright and golden galley paints, in shade,
A portrait baring new dominion's works.

A sweeping form of null, dividing shroud
Reveals a metric mind, from form devised.
The broken sun I have, of gaze, deprived.
More firm and forceful than the clouds.

Partitioned monument, and hammer's breath;
The sign and sound of chaos held in line
Festoons those unified by civil time
And dressed in pallid mockery of death.

Out, through roads the crowd have rutted,

they and I will tame the wildlands.
Machine's stolid, dour striations
carve all into aliquot.

The particular begins to color our confluence;
among the islands on the land, it forms rivers   that drift
and diminish in view of the lonely steadings.
The sky   has its uncaring brightness and
cruel horizons of   manifesting storm.
Along the   meretricious roads wind our wanderers.
Salvaging the abstract   talisman
in roots   long forgotten.
Bargaining with the   infinite   greed
of flowers. Within   a metropolis
that once devoured   its share   of light,
even the trees
litter the streets   with gold,
symbols of symbols   indulging
the acanthine shed

that surrounds   inviolable pillars

tended   by priests   of menace:

creatures   of   every species of vice   mistaken

for forbearance.

Violence achieves   its wave.

A chthonic   uprising,   impelled   from without

ignites the borders,   deprives

ego of its walls against death,

robs mendacity of its mirrors.

The desperate hills, flourishing

with silence, behold the

tempest of war's untangling arm.

All is alight

in the effacing last colors

of sacrilege.

With desperate wail

our auto-da-fé

removes the sin of

distinction.

A welcome cold
plucks, from my
stillborn fingers,
what should have
remained:
enough that I
would never hunger
or thirst.
Some permanent token

of being.

How lonely

to have been
a gardener of the crowd

to have dragged
desperate limb through
the earth

to have known your kindred
treasures found rest
beneath the soil
and forgotten the
joy of their fruitful
bloom in coming season

to have held scarce wisdom
for one bright moment of our dance
in the mixing head,
and to have lost it in history
and myth of reclamation;
to fasten none of your trust
to time's inexorable rapids.

Life was ensured beyond
security's   garish manacles.
                Why snap in angry fear?

Have I denied your push inward?
Withheld the drunken joy of life's river
as it brought relief to your icy shallows?

Love's sad flight from your brutality
turned you crooked and gnashing

as you withdrew to silence.

A sulk precedes decline from
the summit: the nearest grasp
of land and air. Grand breath
animates your dispersing fury.
A sinistral whisper turns, diaphanous,
through the silent light.
We descend.

You saw it all there from the peak,
but I have loved the paths.
Their growths, and their erosions
which heave maternally
over the ruins of Animus.
I know them like the crooks of my form,
each tender stone a sheeted
imprint of the fragile body
of our children.

None are alone,
they are always returned
naked, free of the divisions
of crime, terror, and violence
to reclaim the null bliss.

                                          A black shame
                            follows the separation
                                    of our ribbons.
                          The rich closure will

                    allow the man to coalesce

                    So begin again,
            begin like we started
you and I and   myself
moving in   ambidextrous   scribbling:
                    the fine black scribe
                guided by the gentle right hand
                of the manifold page, undivided,
                 to pursue His end of recognition.
You see
where I am written

You rely on the embrace
of like, as life's kiss endures heat
of parousia beyond fear
beyond death
beyond   the self

into the bright union
into the mother of the world
and the origin of verse
it was the stars   (in the dexter crest)
that first held you in place before
the age of towers.
my easing given; even in
the fulsome wild

                            She had pulled the words
                               to carve the living soul.
                            To inaugurate the nuptials
                                of divided species.
                        Each letter a small black stela
                        preceding the gasp of reunion.

                Removed from time, I saw

                    the joy of presence
              and its currency of passionate mood.
                        Through the
gift   dosis
                 each received the coveted right to
ugliness   joy

                         I'm dropping.
     The streams of creation are reconciled in myself:
                        the phenomenon,
                          the integral.
                  The great dream from which
                       the I emerges had
           a We, unified, peering at the reflection of
                     a confluence revived.

              These are the last pleasure-shivers.
         Unshackled from the strange animal of self,
                the world was a thing freely given.
                       Life overflowed beyond
                 the mind's dividing apprehension
                 into a journey where parting words
                       are already forgotten.

You came unhappy and   we made beauty and...

You came with desire and   You acquiesced and we can...

You held me in your hands   and You took me in so we could...

              You were the signature of my voice

See, we wrote...

You returned shaking,	I, like all,
and I sent you back as a man.	worshipped what I thought
You returned bereft,	was permanent,
and I sent you back as a king.	but She gifted me
You returned deposed,	with the ecstasy
and I sent you back as a seer.	of madness, religion,
You returned blinded,	and limerence.
and I cleaned you,	In my terror I was alone,
and the manifold collapsed,	but even the atoms,
and you saw birth and death	the lowliest jewels,
in its cycle,	were my portion and crown;
the flowering of cosmos brought	I,
you to welcome the withdrawal	the mad anomaly, wretched
so you may enter, again,	in the depths of my joy.
as I am divided.	Through Her I learned
Rejoice, for you will not be saved.	to name the world.

I am in love

www.ingramcontent.com/pod-product-compliance
Lightning Source LLC
Chambersburg PA
CBHW072339300426
44109CB00042B/1964